A CAREER AS AN

ELECTRICIAN

Jobs for
REBUILDING AMERICA™

A CAREER AS AN
ELECTRICIAN

JEFF MAPUA

Rosen
YA™
New York

Published in 2019 by The Rosen Publishing Group, Inc.
29 East 21st Street, New York, NY 10010

Copyright © 2019 by The Rosen Publishing Group, Inc.

First Edition

Library of Congress Cataloging-in-Publication Data

Names: Mapua, Jeff, author.
Title: A career as an electrician / Jeff Mapua.
Description: New York : Rosen Publishing, 2019 | Series: Jobs for rebuilding America | Includes bibliographical references and index. | Audience: Grades 7–12.
Identifiers: LCCN 2017053563| ISBN 9781508179962 (library bound) | ISBN 9781508179979 (pbk.)
Subjects: LCSH: Electrical engineering—Vocational guidance—Juvenile literature. | Electricians—Juvenile literature.
Classification: LCC TK159 .M36 2019 | DDC 621.3023—dc23
LC record available at https://lccn.loc.gov/2017053563

Manufactured in the United States of America

CONTENTS

Georgina came home one evening and noticed something strange. She flipped on the switch to her bedroom lights, and the light bulbs flickered on and off. The light coming from them was also dimmer than normal. She had just put in new light bulbs, so she knew that they were not the problem. The lights in the other rooms were working fine, so Georgina also knew that the electricity was working in her home. Whom could she turn to for help?

The superintendent of her apartment building, Juan, was working in her apartment and installed a new light fixture in the kitchen. He was happy with the way it looked and went to turn it on. Juan noticed that the light switch was warm to the touch. He also noticed that the light fixture was beginning to get warm to the touch. Though he was sure he had installed everything correctly, he was rightfully concerned about his safety and Georgina's. He did not want to risk creating a fire hazard.

Electricians keep the power on in different industry sectors, and they work on homes, office buildings, shopping malls, and more.

For both Georgina and Juan, the answer to their questions was the same. They needed to contact an electrician to help with their problem. Georgina's problem could be the result of a poor connection in her home's electrical circuit. Not addressing the issue could lead to even more severe problems. Juan was correct in being concerned for safety. His problem is a common electrical issue that needs to be addressed as soon as possible.

The next day, Juan called in Walter, an electrician he often used for small jobs. Within fifteen minutes of his arrival at Georgina's, Walter had identified the problem, cut through a section of wall, and pretty soon the new light fixture was working just fine.

The work of electricians is crucial to the infrastructure of the United States. A well-maintained infrastructure keeps the power on, makes travel possible and safe, and is essential to the economy and the public's health. It is important to many aspects of people's lives.

There are many types of electricians. Many work in specialized industry sectors, which require special training and education. Electricians work on private homes, shopping malls, warehouses, office buildings, and other commercial sector structures. They focus on wiring systems and heavy machinery used for commercial projects. This could also include installation and repair of audio and video wiring systems and security systems. Whether they are working on new construction or helping fix old or faulty wiring and lighting in older buildings, electricians keep the power on and flowing for many of the things we need to do.

CHAPTER ONE

BEING AN ELECTRICIAN

*B*eing an electrician can mean undertaking many different types of jobs, tasks, and projects. Electricians who work on wiring big new real estate developments will have different experiences from those whom residents call when the lights go out in a house or apartment. It can be a challenging profession, but a rewarding and well-compensated one.

WHAT DO ELECTRICIANS DO?

A residential electrician can help address issues at a person's home. There are a handful of common repairs and services these electricians encounter on a regular basis. This could be interrupted electrical service, flickering lights, dead or unresponsive outlets, and general updates to a system. Perhaps a home's circuit breakers are constantly tripping, or shutting off the electrical flow to protect the circuit from overheating and causing damage. An electrician will fix the underlying issue, which in this case usually means a circuit that is drawing too much electricity. Overloading a

Blackouts can be caused by a number of different problems or issues. Often, many electricians will work simultaneously during such situations to restore power.

circuit poses a serious threat for starting a fire and needs to be addressed immediately.

Generally speaking, however, electricians are responsible for installing, maintaining, and repairing electrical systems. This includes communications, lighting, and control systems in various locations, including private homes and businesses, and various public and private facilities. Electricians of all types also typically have similar duties, including reading blueprints or technical diagrams, inspecting components such as circuit breakers, and using tools and equipment to diagnose problems and make repairs.

Electricians install wiring and fixtures during the construction of new structures. Others handle rewiring and modernizing old structures, such as stores, workshops,

A picture of a brightly lit city skyline can give you an idea of how much electricians manage.

hospitals, and military and other government buildings. New projects begin with planning and studying the blueprints of whatever structure is being constructed. Electricians wire entire structures. When it comes time to put a plan into effect, electricians will run the necessary cables and wires in a way that works best for the facility, which usually means cables and wiring underground, behind the walls, and in between floors.

Installation of lighting systems includes more than just fixtures. Electricians also install dimmers, switch boxes, and special sockets for appliances such as refrigerators. If a new structure also requires outside lights, the electrician is responsible for those as well.

Maintaining equipment and electrical systems is usually more challenging than installing new ones. Maintenance involves locating and identifying problems that are not as simple as they initially appear. Once the issue is located, sometimes the broken equipment is difficult to reach and repair.

Electricians often employ power tools and specialized equipment in their work. In addition to common construction tools such as screwdrivers, drills, and saws, electricians may use power tools such as conduit benders that run and protect wiring or wire strippers. Other specialized tools include ammeters, voltmeters, and cable testers. They use these and others to help find problems and ensure that equipment is working as it should.

TYPES OF ELECTRICIANS

Inside electricians maintain and repair large motors, equipment, and control systems for businesses and factories. A facility's electrical safety and efficiency are their responsibility. Sometimes, inside electricians install a business's or factory's wiring as it is being built. Inside electricians must also perform regularly scheduled maintenance to keep the systems and equipment running smoothly.

Another type of electrician is a residential electrician. This type of electrician installs and maintains the electrical systems found in people's homes of all different sizes. Residential

Linemen, who are dispatched to fix problems with the grid, are perhaps one of the most familiar sights people think of when they imagine electrical workers.

electricians are involved with the construction of new homes by installing outlets and providing access to power where applicable. For electricians involved with home maintenance and remodeling, duties include repairing and replacing equipment, such as a circuit breaker, when necessary.

Installation electricians are similar to residential ones but usually work on larger projects. These include new construction, like office buildings, stadiums, hospitals, schools, and more. Big projects like this can often take months or years, which is good for contractors, who rely on work outside of the nine-to-five, salaried environment.

Another class of electrical workers is lineman electricians. This type of electrician installs distribution and transmission lines to deliver electricity from its source to customers. For example, a lineman electrician can work for the power company and be responsible for connecting a new home to the nearest power station. Other typical duties include maintaining power lines, climbing poles and transmission towers to string power lines or perform inspections, or identifying defective components such as voltage regulators, transformers, and switches.

WORK ENVIRONMENTS

A minority of electricians are self-employed. The U.S. Bureau of Labor Statistics (BLS) found that in 2014, about one in ten electricians worked for himself or herself. Working for oneself presents a different set of challenges from working for a company. Those who are self-employed are usually residential or residential construction electricians. Many of the aspects of the work environment are the same regardless of whether the electrician is self-employed or not.

An electrician's work environment changes from project to project. Work can take place both indoors and outdoors, requiring different types of equipment.

Electricians will have to work both indoors and outdoors. No two projects are exactly the same. An electrician might be outside one day, then inside the next. A project could be minutes away from one's home or require a long commute to get there.

An electrician's work environment is often physically challenging. Rarely will an electrician sit in a chair all day. Instead, this kind of work requires lots of standing, moving, sitting, kneeling, crouching, and whatever else it takes to complete the task. Cramped, tight spaces are a common characteristic of the work environment.

The BLS also found that electricians suffer from a higher rate of injuries and illnesses than the average worker. Luckily, fatal injuries are unusual. More typical occupational risks can include electrical shocks, falls, burns, cuts, and other minor injuries.

Heavy machinery and power tools used by nearby workers can cause hearing problems. Electricians require protective gear to protect their hearing from damaging noise, as well as gloves to protect their hands, safety glasses for their eyes, hard hats for their heads, and thick work clothes to defend against jagged edges and other pitfalls.

TYPICAL WORK CONDITIONS AND HOURS

One benefit of being an independent contractor electrician is the ability to set one's own schedule. For electricians who work for a company, the hours are generally full time or at least forty hours a week. Working evenings and weekends is also a possibility. Residential electricians, for example, may need to work inside someone's home and he or she could be available only on a weekend. The weather can also play a major role in determining an electrician's work schedule. It may not be safe or possible for an electrician to repair certain equipment in rainy or snowy conditions. Projects can require electricians to work overtime, particularly during scheduled maintenance or on construction sites.

Electricians often work alone. Still, there are times when they must work with others. Other types of specialists, such as elevator installers or people who work on air conditioning and heating systems, will likely have more knowledge about a specific project or equipment than an electrician. These specialists can lend their expertise to ensure that electrical or power systems are installed safely.

Electricians may also need to work closely with building engineers and architects to help with installing and maintaining systems in a new building. Outside of consulting with experts in other fields, if you are part of the construction sector, you will often work with crews of fellow electricians on jobs. These crews generally take on projects too large in scope for a single person to handle. Electricians can also work with assistants or apprentices who help them complete jobs, providing these usually younger workers will valuable feedback and guidance.

BEING A PRO

In March 2012, electrical supervisor William Frierson shared his thoughts with College Recruiter, an employment website, about what it is like being a professional electrician. He oversees employees who install electrical wiring in new commercial buildings and structures. At the time of the interview, he had been a supervisor for three years.

After years of unsatisfying work in another field, Frierson enrolled in a trade school to learn to be an electrician. He said that getting a specialized education, as he did, is far preferable to trying to start as a laborer. He said it was the "best decision that I have ever made." His one piece of advice is to be alert at all times. He has learned to trust his instincts, but his skills and awareness help him stay safe and focused.

Frierson has worked in other fields but finds electrical work to be the most rewarding of them all. Due to the long hours he keeps, the job he loves has come at the expense of some personal time. But he loves what he does for a living and feels that he has found his calling in life.

On a scale of one to ten, with ten denoting the most satisfaction, he rates his position as an eight. "My score only falls a few points short of perfect because of the high levels of stress associated with the position," Frierson said. "There is nothing that can be done to prevent that, however."

NOT AN EASY JOB

An electrician's work environment can sometimes be physically challenging, even cramped or uncomfortable. Electricians might work in confined places, stay on their feet all day, or endure heat and sun outdoors. While one of the obvious dangers is electrocution, other mishaps seem to result in more injuries. Electricity powers our homes, but it can be deadly. Electric shocks can cause a minor jolt and, in more serious cases, can cause cardiac arrest or a heart attack. Construction-related

Faulty wiring and other electrical issues are among the most common causes of residential fires. Electricians can help prevent property damage and loss of life in many situations.

deaths can also be caused by electrocution. Simply touching a live power line risks any of these injuries. It is important for electricians to follow safety guidelines.

Due to electricity's importance in modern society, the effects of power outages can vary from simple inconvenience to life-threatening emergencies, such as when hospitals or emergency services lack the power they need. Clients and customers can be difficult to work with, particularly when they are frustrated with their situations. Many people expect power to be restored as soon as possible. For businesses, a day (or even an hour) without power means lost money. Good electricians make themselves available whenever possible and make the repairs as quickly as they can, with safety as the number-one priority.

CHAPTER TWO

SKILLS FOR SUCCESS

What are the right skills and traits that make a good electrician? Answering these questions can help potential candidates determine if the career is right for them. There are specific skills that most electricians share. On the other hand, someone who would like to pursue a career as an electrician may want to develop certain skills and improve on their weaknesses.

GETTING PHYSICAL

Jobs and projects an electrician undertakes can be physically demanding. An electrician may need to use shovels to dig trenches or use saws to install tubes or troughs for protecting electric wiring called conduits. Both of those tasks and many others like them require at least a little bit of physical ability and stamina.

Stamina means being able to move around and work effectively throughout the day. It means not just being able to physically do the job and not tire out too much, but also to keep your mental faculties sharp. A job could be,

Typical gear associated with electricians includes hard hats, tools like voltmeter cordless drills, screwdrivers, hammers, and much more.

for example, running wire all day or connecting fixtures such as lights, ceiling fans, or exit signs to the wire. Time-consuming and repetitive tasks are par for the course, and it is easy to let exhaustion distract you and make an unfortunate, and even fatal, mistake. Many jobs will require an electrician to climb up and down stairs or ladders for much of the workday.

Electricians also need to have some degree of physical strength. Some fixtures can be heavy or unwieldy and difficult to move. For example, an electrician could be in charge of attaching an antenna to a building's exterior. The antenna could be extremely heavy. Some electric components can weigh fifty pounds (twenty-three kilograms) or more. Lifting them overhead, particularly when working with fixtures that hang from ceilings, means using strength and manual dexterity to move them into the right spot.

Another physical quality that is helpful for electricians is having strong and dexterous, or skillful, hands. Having such hands, coupled with hand-eye coordination, is crucial for this job. Besides formal training, you may be able to improve these skills by taking apart small electronic appliances at home, building models (like airplanes or cars), or even by playing video games.

Good vision is also key. Wearing glasses or contacts is perfectly acceptable as long as they can be worn while performing various tasks. However, being colorblind, a vision disability in which certain colors cannot be distinguished from one another, could make it difficult to perform some assignments. Electrical wires are often color coded and seldom labeled any other way. Not being able to tell which wire is which can lead to wiring

Dealing with outdoor equipment, like large satellite dishes or other gear, requires electricians to be physically fit and agile. They must also often deal with weather extremes throughout the year.

mistakes, which could eventually lead to injuries. About 8 percent of the male population is colorblind and .5 percent of females, according to the National Institutes of Health (NIH). Without a workaround to this disability, such as special glasses or a system that does not rely on colors, being an electrician could prove difficult.

Electricians of all ages have been successfully installing electrical systems and making repairs for many years. When an electrician's project requires fitting into tight, small spaces or getting to hard-to-reach corners, it is helpful for him or her to be physically healthy. This does not mean that all electricians have to be as fit as a professional bodybuilder, but having a full range of motion and the ability to be on one's feet all day is helpful to have.

PERSONALITY TRAITS

According to many occupational advisers, electricians need to have a realistic personality. What traits do they associate with that? One of the most important is a fondness for working with tools or machines. Realistic people also tend to see themselves as practical and mechanical. They tend not to dwell on setting goals that could be considered fanciful, impossible, or long shots. Being sensible means making wise choices that are likely to benefit oneself or others and working towards one's goals slowly, in a methodical manner. Someone with a realistic personality type values things that are practical and can be seen and touched. These could be things such as plants and animals, which are grown or raised, or things that can be built and improved upon. Realistic personality types do not fear getting their hands dirty while doing their jobs.

There are other nontechnical skills an electrician should have or try to develop to achieve career success. According to O*NET, a provider of career-related data services, electricians pay close attention to details. This means making sure that every step is taken care of when completing a task and paying close attention to one's surroundings and area. An electrician's

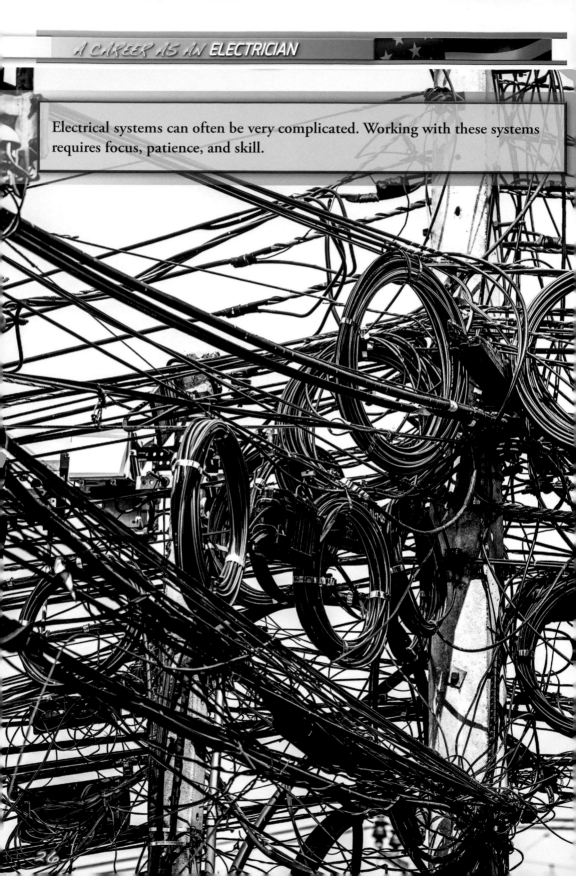

Electrical systems can often be very complicated. Working with these systems requires focus, patience, and skill.

work style also displays leadership—in other words, taking responsibility and control over projects and tasks. Similarly, successful electricians are able to work independently and take initiative without the need for another person to assign tasks and set goals. O*NET also describes electricians as capable of handling stress and working in a cooperative, honest environment.

Dependability is an important trait in any job, but an essential one for electricians. People rely on having the power on to go about their daily routines, and outages can be both disruptive and life threatening. Clients and others should be able to rely on an electrician diagnosing a problem, making a reasonable estimate of what needs to be done to fix it, and then going about it in a dependable, straightforward, and honest way.

Electricians should also be patient and in control of their emotions. Problems will arise during projects, either from the equipment, the work itself, or from other people involved. It can sometimes be difficult to work with others, especially if they have a difference of opinion regarding how a goal should be accomplished. It is important for an electrician to stay focused on the task at hand and accept work delays or a change in plans without getting angry and losing control.

CORE SKILLS

General business skills are important not just for electricians but for all professionals. Many electricians may go on to own their own businesses. They will have to seek new work, bid on jobs, track inventory, organize payroll, and assign work and tasks to others. Good people skills are also essential when interacting with clients and other contractors on job sites. A friendly electrician is more likely to earn and retain customers.

There are other useful skills for electricians that go beyond one's physical abilities or personality characteristics. These can be divided into six categories: communication, mathematics, information technology, work with others, improvements in one's own learning, and problem solving.

On the job, electricians will be faced with many different situations. New issues and problems arise that must be resolved in a creative way. Troubleshooting —the ability to locate faults and make repairs in a mechanical or electronic system—is one of the most important parts of the job. Electricians often encounter a failing component and must find, diagnose, and then repair whatever is causing the problem. For example, if the lighting in a wing of a school building is flickering, an electrician can perform tests to find what is causing this to occur. Once located, the issue can then be addressed.

THE NATIONAL ELECTRIC CODE (NEC)

Electrical work is heavily regulated, and electricians, no matter what state they work in, must adhere to specific procedures and rules while on the job. These codes are in place to ensure the safety of the electrician and his or her customers. Over time, an experienced electrician will know many of these rules by heart.

In the United States, the standard for safe installation of electrical wiring and equipment is called the National Electric Code, or NEC, and is part of the larger National Fire Codes, established by the National Fire Protection Association (NFPA). The NEC was first published in 1897. It was developed to address a rash of electrical fires in the late nineteenth century. Many of the buildings destroyed by such fires were textile mills and other industrial facilities.

The NEC provides members of the electrical sector—including workers, regulators, inspectors, and others—with a central resource to refer to. It is updated every three years to incorporate new developments, innovations, and changes to federal law. In book form, the NEC is about one thousand pages long and is also available online at the NFPA website. It is not meant to be an instruction manual. Electricians often call the NEC the electrician's bible because of its importance in safeguarding people and property from the dangers posed by electricity and its systems.

Building schematics, blueprints, diagrams, and other visual and written materials are part of the job of being an electrician.

SCIENCE AND MATH

Many hands-on careers require a basic or even intermediate grasp of mathematics. Electricians do not necessarily need to be mathematical experts. For example, they do not need to solve complex equations or understand advanced theorems. However, they need to be able to handle basic concepts involving whole numbers, fractions, and decimal points. The basic operations are addition, subtraction, multiplication, and division. For example, voltage, current, and resistance are some of the basic properties on the job that will need to be figured out using mathematics. While some people are naturals at math, others must put work into improving their skills in this subject area.

Algebra is a major branch of mathematics that can really inform an electrician's duties. It uses letters and symbols to represent numbers in formulas and equations. Electricians must be able to rearrange formulas to solve various problems involving electrical quantities and values. For example, the formula for calculating current is I = P/E, where I equals the current, P equals the power such as wattage, and E equals the voltage. If an electrician knows the power value and the voltage, he or she can figure out the current.

Modern electrical grids are often complex and must be overseen by teams that watch carefully for failures in the system.

There are many other formulas that an electrician must understand to complete various jobs. These could be the formula for the area, or amount of surface, of an object, or the conversion of one type of measurement, such as meters, into another, such as feet. For example, an electrician could measure the length of a component, like a wire, in feet. However, many blueprints and building plans represent distances and lengths in meters. The ability to convert such measurements on the fly is important for electricians.

CHAPTER THREE

EDUCATION AND TRAINING

Those interested in an electrician's career have a lot of training and hard work ahead, with a great payoff. That payoff is entrance into an interesting and vital profession that all members of society rely on daily. Licenses and certifications are required to perform certain tasks, and the way to get them is via intensive training and on-the-job learning.

EDUCATION

Electricians are expected to have a high school diploma or it equivalent. After high school, future electricians can pursue a variety of degrees and certifications from technical schools and colleges, and community colleges.

These two-year programs teach students valuable skills, including building, operating, and maintaining electrical equipment. Courses and exact topics covered will vary from school to school, but students should expect to learn about motors and controllers used in manufacturing and the generating and distribution equipment used to make

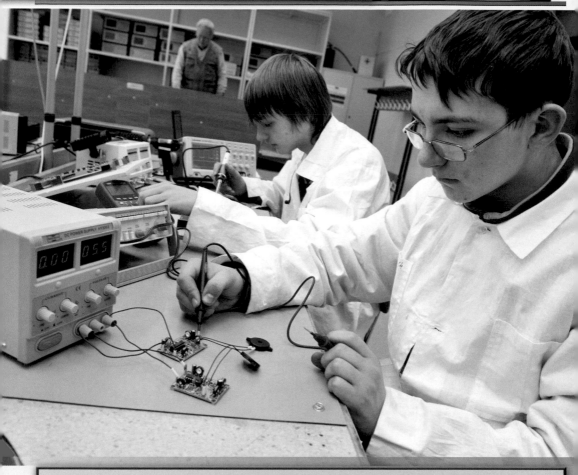

Getting exposure to electronics early on—such as in an electronics, engineering, or shop course of some kind—is a great way to see if electrician is a career you would be interested in pursuing.

electricity. Programs offered at technical schools are related to topics such as circuitry, safety practices, and basic electrical information. After earning a technical degree, graduates usually receive credit to use toward their time as apprentices.

Four-year degree programs are also available for those interested in becoming electricians. A degree in electrical engineering, for example, will prepare students for designing entire systems. Electrical engineering degrees help students develop skills related to physical technologies, hardware and software systems, and information technology. Using physics and mathematical theories and tools, electrical engineers also learn how to develop smart electric grids, wired and wireless communications systems, and much more. Course topics and subjects include math, computing, electronics, and physical sciences, such as chemistry, physics, and earth sciences. With a degree, students should gain technical knowledge along with the ability to communicate well with others.

Continuing education courses are another option for those seeking to learn new skills and put them to work. Continuing education includes classes outside the community college or four-year college or university setting. Many adults who are already in the middle of their careers take such classes to develop new skills, train for entirely new jobs, earn additional or supplementary degrees, or follow personal interests or passions. For electricians, continuing education means professional development, earning a certificate or license, or earning college credit. The courses they take help them stay abreast of safety practices, updates to the electrical code, and train to use and maintain specific products and tools.

Professional development course topics can also include introductions to software such as Excel or other business applications, lessons on professionalism, or specialized training on equipment such as transformers or conductors. Earning college credit generally involves taking courses intended for those pursuing a degree. Courses could be in electrical engineering or a physical science.

Continuing studying electrical systems and electronics as part of a college degree program or enrolling in a vocational-technical school or technical college are both paths to an electrician's career.

APPRENTICESHIP AND TRAINING

Outside of the educational environment, most electricians learn how to do the job through an apprenticeship program. Most states actually require two to four years as an apprentice before anyone can receive official licensing to do electrical work. Apprentice electricians shadow, or work alongside, veteran, licensed ones.

Some contractors provide their own training programs. These are separate from an apprenticeship and are not recognized as such. However, a training program through an electrical employer can include both classroom work and the on-the-job training that is so important to an electrician's career. There are even training programs that can precede an apprenticeship. These are for electricians who have been working as helpers. The Home Builders Institute offers a pre-apprenticeship certificate training (PACT) program. In fact, electrician is just one of eight trades covered under the PACT program.

To qualify for an apprenticeship, apprentices must be at least eighteen years old. A high school diploma or its equivalent is required as is the completion of one year of algebra. In addition, apprentices must take an aptitude test and earn a qualifying score. An aptitude test determines a person's ability or knowledge of a particular skill. Finally, apprentices must also pass a substance abuse screening.

An apprenticeship program can last four to five years and usually covers a minimum number of hours of training and work experience. Each year of a program might require apprentices to complete at least 144 hours of technical training and 2,000 hours of paid on-the-job training. Technical training includes classroom hours. There, apprentices learn about various subjects related to the profession, such as electrical theory, blueprint reading, electrical code requirements, safety, and first aid. Classes also provide specialized training for soldering, a method of melting metal or a mixture of metals to join metal objects together.

UNION AND NONUNION APPRENTICESHIPS

Unions and other professional associations sponsor apprenticeship programs. They provide the financial support and guidance to allow the apprentice to concentrate on learning the trade. Some apprenticeship programs give precedence to the applications of veterans of the military ahead of other candidates.

A labor union is an organization of workers formed to protect the rights of its members, including their wages, benefits, and working conditions. Two groups, the International Brotherhood of Electrical Workers (IBEW) and the National Electrical Contractors Association (NECA), together established the Electrical Training Alliance. This is a program that provides union apprenticeships. Apprentices are paired with a local union employer until licensing requirements are met. Being a union apprentice also requires becoming a member of the IBEW.

Nonunion apprenticeships are also available. They are through nonunion employers, sometimes called open shops or merit shops. The two major organizations that provide and place apprentices with nonunion employers are the Independent Electrical Contractors (IEC) and Associated Builders and Contractors, Inc. (ABC). Both of these bodies have branches in many major cities and regions across the United States and use their branches to pair apprentices with nonunion contractors in the area. Following the completion of an apprenticeship, electricians must then pass their journeyman electrician

Younger electricians often work with more experienced ones within the framework of an apprenticeship.

examination. Completing an apprenticeship also qualifies the person to do other construction and maintenance work.

JOURNEYMAN

The next step following apprenticeships is becoming a journey worker or journeyman. A journeyman is a licensed tradesperson and works for an employer. Journeymen are able to perform duties on their own that fall under their local or state licensing requirements. Other times, journeymen must have their work supervised or approved by a master electrician.

However, earning a journeyman license requires fulfilling a specific number of experience hours depending on local and state rules. Generally, one year of education counts as one thousand hours of on-the-job experience. Candidates for journeyman status can apply up to two years of education, or two thousand hours, toward their certification. The remaining hours of experience, if not earned via an apprenticeship, must therefore be gained through on-the-job training. A school can provide assistance finding work placements to complete those hours.

Journeyman electrician examinations are administered via local jurisdictions. Those who are ready to take the exam should apply through their appropriate state, regional, county, or city government regulatory agency. Proof of completion of the classroom and on-the-job training hours is required at this point. In Texas, for instance, test takers must have at least eight thousand hours of on-the-job training under the supervision of a master electrician. Although registration is done through a local government agency, the actual exams are conducted by a testing company.

Every jurisdiction has its own version of the electrical exam. Test takers should prepare for multiple-choice questions and to spend between three to fours hours in the exam room. Some areas even offer open-book exams and require a grade of 70 percent or higher to pass. Subjects covered can include any number of topics. These can include general electrical knowledge,

The International Brotherhood of Electrical Workers (IBEW) is one of the biggest unions that electricians belong to and coordinates skills training and apprenticeships for many in the sector every year.

feeder circuits, communication systems, special occupancies, low-voltage electrical systems, and electricity safety. Material covering local electrical codes and safety standards, which will vary among jurisdictions, may be included as well.

In Texas, for example, the journeyman exam consists of eighty questions and the test is administered over four hours. Many topics are covered, including services, wiring methods, switchboards, motors and generators, conductors, and more. A score of 75 percent is considering a passing grade. To even take the exam, test takers must have at least eight thousand hours of on-the-job training under the supervision of a master electrician.

LICENSES AND CERTIFICATIONS

Earning a certificate or license is a significant milestone for an electrician. One major step is when someone passes the journeyman electrician exam. The license that person gains at this step permits electricians to work on residential and commercial projects, performing tasks like wiring, installing, and repairing electrical equipment. These are all jobs that can be performed without direct supervision, although such work will usually be done as part of a team led by a master electrician.

Journeyman licenses need to be periodically renewed. States may require different types of licenses for different types of work. For example, a specific license could be required for residential or commercial projects, specialty installations, or for work at industrial facilities.

The terms "license" and "certification" are sometimes used interchangeably by different states. Electricians are encouraged

NATIONAL ELECTRICAL CONTRACTORS ASSOCIATION

The National Electrical Contractors Association (NECA) began in 1901 as a group of electrical contractors who came together to address the issues that their new industry was facing. They fostered trade and reformed the abuses that they had experienced. The goal was to not only help the electrical industry, but also to protect the public from substandard work and to foster innovation.

NECA is a membership organization. Its contractors try to provide solutions for their customers as well as provide their electrical expertise to those involved with construction projects. They also set industry standards for both traditional and integrated electrical systems. NECA aims to be the industry leader in the application of new technologies. Members receive many benefits, including education, training, and business and market development. NECA also holds their own events for contractors to meet others in their field as well as learn about the latest news concerning electricians.

Members of NECA form committees and task forces to determine and shape the organization's programs and policy proposals. As technology is constantly evolving, so too must NECA and their processes. NECA's CEO directs the overall direction of these efforts.

to check carefully what is required of them in their home states. For example, in New York there is no state licensing of contractors or journeymen. However, New York City requires licensing. Apprentices are not licensed, but a master electrician is. Becoming a master electrician has its own set of requirements, such as 3.5 years of experience, a bachelor's degree in engineering, and more.

CHAPTER FOUR

PURSUING A CAREER

Obtaining an electrician's license is an accomplishment in itself—one that someone should be proud of. However, it is just the first step. Finding work independently as a contractor or as one of a company's employees is the next step in launching a career. Many people know early on what sector of electrical work they will enter, though some may try out one or more until they find the right fit. Electricians may pursue niche specialties, though many make an effort to be well rounded.

WORKING FOR A UTILITY

Electrical power is produced or generated by a utility, or power plant. Electricians in this sector are in charge of maintaining and repairing generators. For example, a hydroelectric plant converts the energy from water flowing from a reservoir or river through a dam to generate electrical energy. Utility branch electricians then distribute

Utilities, such as this power plant, will likely have a dedicated staff of electricians or technicians on hand to address electrical problems as they arise.

the power the plant generates. This is commonly done via the overhead transmission lines that can be seen on many streets.

A utility company responsible for generating electricity can service an area more than 100 square miles (161 square kilometers). Millions of customers depend on their regional power plants to obtain electricity through a network of substations and regional maintenance centers. Emergency help responding to power outages can be deployed quickly via local branches rather than from central utilities.

Utility companies provide jobs for thousands of people across the country. Different positions include maintenance electricians, line workers, troubleshooters, and cable splicers. Cable splicing is when two electrical wires are joined together.

CONSTRUCTION

Whenever buildings or other structures are being built, electricians make up an essential part of the crew. Their jobs involve working with wires, conduits, and current to install, connect, and test electrical wiring systems within the new building or structure.

Construction electricians also provide initial hookups for the parts of the heating, ventilation, and air conditioning (HVAC) systems that require power. If the new building is a residence, such as a house, construction electricians may also install common appliances, such as a hot-water tank, dishwasher, or a washing machine.

Working on a new building can be considered either rough work or finish work. Jobs done during the final stages of construction are considered finish work. For example, if an electrician installs a light fixture in a room that has already been built, it would be considered finish work since it is the last step in the process. Finish work enhances service and aesthetic features. Installing the wiring inside the walls and ceiling to power that same light fixture would be considered rough work.

Newer construction, such as this modern apartment complex, often adheres to low-energy and green environmental codes. Electricians must be familiar with the latest standards and trends.

Rough work occurs much earlier in the construction process than finish work.

MAINTENANCE

Once electrical systems are installed, they must then be maintained. Maintenance electricians are different from construction electricians because they work on already existing systems. They focus less on installation and testing processes and more on preserving what is there and ensuring it remains operational. Whether this requires the maintenance electrician to repair or completely replace equipment, the responsibility of keeping the power running lies with him or her.

The work could involve the wiring or any piece of electrical equipment. Maintenance electricians also consult blueprints and diagrams to better understand the systems they work on. Since they may not have been involved with the installation, these blueprints and diagrams can help tremendously in maintaining equipment. They also use specialized tools, such as meters and other test equipment, to locate any issues that need addressing.

SPECIAL FIELDS

There are many specific areas in which an electrician can work. These are smaller industry segments with many of their own procedures and specialized equipment to learn. Notable ones include the motor shop industry, working with electric signs, marine and shipboard services, cable television installation and line maintenance, and electronics.

Newer fields are emerging as technology advances, providing even more specialized electrical jobs. These include working with fiber optics, lasers, and robotics. These newer fields also connect electricians with electronics workers. Fiber optics refers to long, thin strands of pure glass or other transparent solids about as wide as human hair. These strands of glass are

With so many different power and communications systems feeding into homes and businesses these days, electricians must be familiar with a wide variety of wiring schemes and setups.

then bundled together into optical cables. The cables are then used to transmit light signals, mostly for telecommunications or for medical purposes to see inside the body.

EXPERIENCE COUNTS

Experience counts when it comes to achieving career milestones like certifications. It also figures in when electricians get new jobs or raises in their current ones. Naturally, an electrician with five to seven years' experience will generally command higher wages than one who is just starting out.

The jobs site Careerbuilder.com notes that electricians with less than a year of experience make up a small portion of the overall industry—about 2 percent. Electricians with one to four years of experience make up 22 percent of the workforce, while electricians with five to nine years of experience make up about 21 percent. At about 31 percent, the largest segment of electricians has between ten and nineteen years of experience. Finally, electricians who have more than twenty years of experience account for about 24 percent of the electrician workforce.

The high number of long-tenured electricians hints at the value placed on having experience. That should not be too surprising since people are depending on an electrician to provide power to their home, office, or workplace. Electricians should feel confident that their careers will hold up over time and that as their expertise grows, their ability to compete in the marketplace will remain strong.

MAKING A DIFFERENCE

Electricians can provide much-needed help in the wake of natural disasters and man-made ones like war. In a surgical hospital in Amman, the capital of Jordan, the medical nonprofit Doctors Without Borders averages about 180 patients on any given day. According to a story in *National Geographic*, the doctors there perform reconstructive surgeries as well as provide long-term care for refugees and survivors from war zones in Syria, Iraq, Yemen, and Israeli-occupied Gaza.

The building was relatively modern, but it was held back by inefficient energy systems and lighting. Its monthly energy bills ran as high as $65,000. That is when an electrician from Eugene, Oregon, named Bryan Garcia was sent to help. Over the course of his seventeen-year career, he had helped people recover from hurricanes in Florida and aided people in Malawi and Sri Lanka.

Garcia installed window films to absorb excess sunlight and help regulate the temperature in the building. He replaced the harsh fluorescent lights with LEDs that gave off a softer, warmer glow, and used 75 percent less energy. In addition, he recommended installing a solar power system that could potentially save the hospital up to $300,000 over a ten-year. Garcia related to *National Geographic,* "It was a good reminder of why we were doing this. These are people who are living in a hospital who have survived some of the most brutal conditions imaginable."

LANDING A JOB

Finding work can be very competitive, especially if an open position is with a highly valued company or in a great location. Luckily, there are many things a person can do to help his or her chances of finding and landing that perfect job. These include looking for work both online and off, combing through trade publications, contacting teachers and mentors, and much more. Networking is a particularly useful tactic. This is the practice of connecting or meeting with people who can be helpful professionally. A little bit of networking—even for those who don't like to do it—can go far, whether it gets someone a new job entirely or helps him or her move up or around in a particular company.

One way to distinguish oneself as a candidate is to earn a specialty license. Such licenses include those that certify the electrician to be an outside wireman, work with solar power, handle refrigeration, or specialize in elevator or escalator

These electricians were dispatched to repair electrical infrastructure in Puerto Rico damaged by Hurricane Maria in September 2017. Much of the island was without power for many weeks.

maintenance and repair. Before looking for work, it would be a good idea to check the local rules for these types of jobs.

One potential route is to become an independent electrical contractor. However, before an electrician can really work completely independently, he or she should achieve the rank of master electrician. As noted, becoming a master electrician requires a high level of experience and education. If an electrician does become independent, it can be a rewarding experience. Many people cherish the flexibility and freedom of being one's own boss. A journeyman might break out on his or her own, but he or she needs to have a client base ready before investing in the sometimes risky route of a small contracting business.

Independent electricians, whatever their level, might depend a great deal on referrals for work. A referral is when an electrician's customer is happy with his or her work and suggests to a friend, relative, or business associate that that person hire that same electrician for his or her purposes. Cultivating relationships with construction contractors, building managers, and others who may one day need an electrician is a good idea. Similarly, once work has been completed, it is helpful to maintain a relationship with a customer. The customer can be more than just a good referral in the future, he or she can also give electricians feedback about what they did well and where they might be able to improve.

Electricians should also subscribe to job or construction bid boards. They usually charge a monthly fee, but they are a good resource for finding work. The boards post local, regional, and national ads for projects that users can then bid on. The federal government also may offer certain projects first to bidders or firms led by women, people of color, or military veterans. These are called set-aside programs and can be found on state or national sites such as setasidealert.com.

The job of an electrician can often be stressful and physically and mentally draining. It helps to unwind, joke around, and build relationships as a way to decompress and make the workday more tolerable.

PROFESSIONAL SKILLS

Beyond the physical and personal qualities that make up a successful electrician are professional skills. These are common across a variety of career paths, underscoring how important they can be to any professional. They can be practiced and improved upon and will come in handy in many situations faced by an electrician out doing a job.

Endurance is the ability to stay focused while maintaining a good level of effort over time. A good electrician can be consistent while also exercising patience and self-control. This means being able to face challenges without losing composure. Persistence, or the ability to work through tough situations like poor weather, is another quality good electricians have.

Getting work done on time requires good time-management skills. This also applies to estimating how long a project will take as well as what it will cost. Employers want to hire someone who can communicate well and work with a team, too. Having people skills is important not only for dealing with coworkers but also customers. This is particularly important for an independent contractor.

In addition, independent electricians, especially when they are first starting out, should make sure their clerical skills are adequate and be well versed in the latest business software. Of course, they must be up to date on the latest electrical codes and procedures. These codes can be difficult to remember but are vitally important both in finding work and carrying out projects.

CHAPTER FIVE

THE ROAD AHEAD

*T*he electrical industry is well over a century old. New technologies and industry-wide standards make it both a dynamic, in-demand, and well-regulated job sector. Will electricians remain in demand? Industry experts can provide their insights about expectations for the future and what it holds in terms of salary and job prospects. New technology could change electricians' duties, too.

JOB OUTLOOK

Today, electricians are in high demand—particularly for maintenance rather than construction purposes. It is expected that electricians will continue to find steady work in the coming years and decades. Older systems need maintenance, repairs, and eventual replacement. Additionally, the technology used in electrical systems is updated and switched out periodically. As many regions move away from fossil fuels to other power sources, electricians will be needed to help with these changes. As a result, continuing education will be an integral part of any electrical career.

The move to retrofit older buildings with newer and greener wiring systems, and the need to build new ones from the ground up, means that electricians will be sought after for decades to come.

Records compiled by the US Bureau of Labor Statistics and other sources show that, as the economy goes, so does employment for electricians. When the economy thrives, people build more buildings and homes. These new structures need electricians to safely install electrical systems and various components. Additionally, electricians will be on hand for maintenance and repairs.

However, when the economy is not doing as well, electricians will find that work is harder to come by. New construction slows down. So competition will be tougher for available jobs since there is not enough work to go around. Maintenance and repairs will be less in demand. The BLS did find that electricians in factories generally have more stable employment than their counterparts in the other industry sectors.

The BLS also counsels electricians to focus on developing a wide skill set. This means being able to perform a variety of different tasks, including electronic systems repair, solar panel installation, and industrial component wiring. The BLS believes those with multiple skills will ultimately have the greatest number of job opportunities. They also note that having a military background can help during the hiring process. Employers may have special programs in place to help veterans and military servicemen find work.

Military servicemen can learn valuable trade skills, such as in electrical work, while performing their service. Upon their return to civilian life, they can take advantage of programs in place to help veterans find work in their fields.

SALARY AND PAY OUTLOOK

According to the BLS, the average wages of electricians make this a comfortably middle-class career path. Apprentices should expect to earn about half of what fully trained electricians make, with appropriate pay raises coming as experience is gained. The manufacturing and power generation branches of the electrical industry generally offer higher wages than their counterparts in construction.

Electricians compare favorably to all other careers after growth projections, salaries, and education are taken into account. According to Yahoo! Finance, electrician is the fifth-best job for the future. In 2013, there were 577,000 electricians in the United States. This number is expected to increase through 2023. The site cites increased electrical connectivity at both homes and offices as a factor in the industry's growth. Increasing use of alternative energies, such as solar and wind, also suggest a bright future for electricians.

REBUILDING INFRASTRUCTURE: THE CHALLENGE AHEAD

Infrastructure refers to the system of public works, including buildings, roads, and power supplies, needed for a city or state to properly operate. In the United States, the repair and upgrading of the country's infrastructure is a major concern for the people and government. The American Society of

Civil Engineers filed a report about America's infrastructure and gave an overall grade of D+. The country's roads, bridges, dams, schools, and other structures all graded poorly, with no single element receiving an A grade. The report stated that there has not been much improvement in America's energy programs or in its transportation, water, or waste management programs.

The US government and its leaders have made numerous proclamations about the importance of improving the country's infrastructure. One such plan was unveiled in December 2016 and included fifty potential projects. The $137.5 billion plan singled out projects involving high-speed rail, airports, and

Electricians will certainly be part of the mix of those called upon to help fix the outdated power grid and aging infrastructure that many states and the federal government need to deal with in the coming years.

subways. However, there were also many plans to improve power and the transmission of electricity across multiple states. The plans cost anywhere from $2.2 billion to $5 billion and include improvements dealing with energy storage, grid modernization, and transmission line improvement.

Other proposed plans cost up to $1 trillion over ten years with goals of repairing and expanding infrastructure. About $1 billion of the estimated cost targets energy infrastructure and grid modernization. There are also tax incentives, or economic encouragements, for improving or using renewable energy, electricity generation, and energy efficiency.

FIVE YEARS

For an electrician five years into his or her career, training should be completed, and he or she will likely have earned a certification. Otherwise, he or she will still be in the phase of an electrician's assistant, while he or she tries to pass local and federal requirements. At this point, electricians may pursue work through sponsoring unions or find work as a subcontractor for one of these groups. A subcontractor is hired by a company or electrician to work on a project that company or electrician has already agreed to. Outside of a guild or union, electricians can find work as on-site maintenance contractors.

In addition, the Princeton Review, a major publisher of college test preparation materials that also tracks career trends, suggests joining a union soon after earning one's certification.

GREEN POWER

While the United States has not been a consistent leader in adopting green or environmentally friendly technologies, other nations have more aggressively pursued alternative energy production. In Europe, governments and private entities continue to invest a great deal in wind and solar energy. China has pumped hundreds of billions of dollars into renewable energy and energy efficiency, positioning the nation as a leader in green innovation. For its part, the United States is home to many of the world's leading technology companies, such as those in Silicon Valley. Such firms are more committed than others.

For the most part, homeowners turn to solar energy as an alternative source of electricity. Wind power, on the other hand, is mostly installed in wind farms of giant turbines that power large-scale systems. However, mini wind turbines might make wind a viable option for the home. Meant to be installed on a flat roof, the turbines can be used alone or as part of a larger array. Each fanlike turbine, six feet (two meters) in diameter, generates an average of 1,500 kilowatt-hours a year, and an average home uses about 11,000 kilowatt-hours a year.

One thing holding back solar panels' popularity is price. Companies are trying to produce them more cheaply, however. Newer, thin-film solar panels use much less silicon than their older counterparts and will likely become an industry standard.

Improving infrastructure also relies on better ways to measure energy used. Traditional electric meters convey only basic information to consumers and utilities. Utilities rely on customers to inform them about power outages. Innovative smart meters can instead alert the power companies immediately of a blackout, giving them an accurate picture of how energy is being used.

Local electrician unions have proven to be a powerful force in the industry.

TEN YEARS

With ten years of experience, an electrician will have established himself or herself as a capable professional. At this point in a career, an electrician should have developed a number of different skills and become an expert in at least one. An electrician's experiences with difficult projects or demanding clients have only made him or her more seasoned. Ten years of making contacts, networking, and perhaps going after new business if the electrician is independent will hopefully have paid off.

Of course, only about 20 percent of electricians form their own contracting or consulting companies. Others may opt to become instructors in apprenticeship programs. For these electricians, the pay may be less than working as a regular electrician, but the hours are usually more favorable and the pay is more consistent.

⊘ Typical entry-level education requirement: high school diploma or equivalent

⊘ Typical training an electrician can expect: four- or five-year apprenticeship, then on-the-job training

⊘ Approximate number of jobs in the United States in 2016: 666,900, with another 60,100 jobs available by 2026

⊘ Expected job outlook through 2026: increase of about 9 percent

⊘ General job description: install, maintain, and repair electrical power, communications, lighting, and control systems in homes, businesses, factories, and other facilities and sites

⊘ Typical duties include: read blueprints or technical diagrams; install and maintain wiring, control, and lighting system; inspect electrical components; identify electrical problems; repair or replace wiring, equipment, or fixtures; follow state, local, and other regulations, using the National Electrical Code; direct and train workers in installation, maintenance, and repair of wiring and equipment

⊘ Job environment: indoor and outdoor work; full-time, including evenings and weekends, depending on the position; on-the-job hazards include electrical shock, burns, cuts, and falls, which electricians experience at higher rates than the national average; working in cramped spaces; requires protective clothing: gloves, safety glasses, and hard hats

apprenticeship A job taken by a novice tradesperson for the purpose of learning under an experienced professional.

aptitude A natural ability or talent for something.

circuit A complete and closed path through which a circulating electric current can flow.

commute To travel back and forth regularly.

conduit A tube or trough used for protecting electric wiring.

dexterous Being skilled with one's hands.

generator A machine that creates energy, such as electricity.

infrastructure The buildings, roads, and other structures and systems, both visible and hidden, that are needed for a society to work efficiently.

journeyman An electrician that has completed an apprenticeship or otherwise has become fully licensed.

network To connect with people who can be helpful professionally, especially in finding employment.

residential Of or relating to the places where people live.

solder A metal or a mixture of metals that is melted to join other metals together.

stamina The ability to sustain physical or mental effort over time.

subcontractor A third party who usually agrees to supply work or materials required in an original contract.

tax incentive A feature of the tax code designed to encourage a particular economic activity.

transformer A device for changing an electric current into one of different voltage.

trip The action taken when a circuit breaker shuts off the electrical flow to protect the circuit from overheating and causing damage.

troubleshoot To locate faults and make repairs in a mechanical or electronic system.

union An organization of workers formed to protect the rights and advance the interests of its members concerning wages, benefits, and working conditions.

utility A business that provides a service, namely energy, under close regulation or even ownership.

Canadian Electrical Contractors Association
41 Maple Street
Uxbridge, ON L9P 1C8
(416) 491-2414
Email: ceca@ceca.org
Website: http://www.ceca.org/index.asp
Twitter: @CECANational
The Canadian Electrical Contractors Association, chartered
in 1955, is a federation of groups, representing more than
eight thousand electrical contractors at the national level.

Canadian Standards Association Group
178 Rexdale Boulevard
Toronto, Ontario M9W 1R3
Canada
(416) 747-4000
Website: http://www.csagroup.org
Facebook: @CSA-Group-113511338721494
Twitter: @CSA_Group
CSA Group provides testing, inspection, and certification
services, including safety and environmental certification
for Canada and the United States.

Electronic Engineering (EE) Times
303 Second Street, South Tower, Suite 900
San Francisco, CA 94107
Website: https://www.eetimes.com
Twitter and Facebook: @eetimes
A global media company covering the electronics industry

since 1972, EE Times runs a network of websites covering the electronics industry.

International Brotherhood of Electrical Workers (IBEW)
900 Seventh Street NW
Washington, DC 20001
(202) 833-7000
Email: webmaster@ibew.org
Website: http://www.ibew.org
Twitter: @IBEW
Facebook: @IBEWFB
IBEW is a union of about 750,000 members in the United States and Canada. It represents those who work for utilities and in construction, telecommunications, broadcasting, manufacturing, railroads, and government.

National Electrical Contractors Association (NECA)
3 Bethesda Metro Center, Suite 1100
Bethesda, MD 20814
(301) 657-3110
Website: http://www.necanet.org
Facebook and Twitter: @NECANET
Instagram: @neca_net
With 119 chapters across the country, NECA is dedicated to helping the electrical industry through research, national representation, and more.

Occupational Safety and Health Administration (OSHA)
200 Constitution Avenue NW
Washington, DC 20210
(800) 321-6742
Website: https://www.OSHA.gov
Twitter: @OSHA_DOL
Facebook: @departmentoflabor
Instagram: @USDOL
OSHA is the main government entity that sets standards for
and enforces rules covering worker safety.

Western Electrical Contractors Association, Inc. (WECA)
3695 Bleckely Street
Rancho Cordova, CA 95655
(916) 453-0112
Email: info@goweca.com
Website: https://www.goweca.com/Home.aspx
Twitter and Facebook: @GOWECA
WECA is a California-based association offering members
political and public affairs efforts, networking, training,
and more. Programs include apprenticeship, training, and
certification classes.

FOR FURTHER READING

Dawson, Patricia. *An Electrician's Job*. New York, NY: Cavendish Square, 2015.

Freedman, Jeri. *Electrician*. New York, NY: Cavendish Square Publishing, 2016.

Goldsworthy, Kaite. *Electricity*. New York, NY: Smartbook Media Inc., 2017.

Herman, Stephen L. *Electronics for Electricians*. Boston, MA: Cengage Learning, 2017.

Hord, Colleen. *From Power Plant to House*. Vero Beach, FL: Rourke Educational Media, 2015.

Houghton Mifflin Harcourt. *On the Job with an Electrician*. Boston, MA: Houghton Mifflin School, 2013.

Institute for Career Research. *Career as an Electrician, Electrical Contractor*. Chicago, IL: Institute for Career Research, 2015.

Labrecque, Ellen. *Electrician*. Ann Arbor, MI: Cherry Lake Publishing, 2017.

Martin, Bobi. *Working as an Electrician in Your Community*. New York, NY: Rosen Publishing, 2016.

Niver, Heather Moore. *Cool Careers Without College for People Who Can Build Things*. New York, NY: Rosen Publishing, 2014.

Rudman, Jack. *Car Equipment Electrician*. Syosset, NY: National Learning Corp., 2014.

Best Jobs: U.S. News and World Report Rankings. "Electrician: Reviews and Advice." *U.S. News & World Report.* Retrieved September 27, 2017. https://money .usnews.com/careers/best-jobs/electrician/reviews.

CareerBuilder. "What Can You Expect from a Job as an Electrician?" September 20, 2016. https://www .careerbuilder.com/advice/what-can-you-expect-from-a -job-as-an-electrician.

Electrician Careers Guide. "Is Electrician a Good Career Choice?" Retrieved September 11, 2017. http://www .electriciancareersguide.com/is-electrician-a-good-career -choice.

Electrician Careers Guide. "Personality Traits and Skills of Successful Electricians." Retrieved September 13, 2017. http://www.electriciancareersguide.com/personality-traits -and-skills-of-successful-electricians.

ElectricianSchoolEdu.org. "How to Become an Electrician." Retrieved September 19, 2017. http://www .electricianschooledu.org.

ElectricianSchoolEdu.org. "State-by-State Electrician License and Certification Requirements at a Glance." Retrieved September 21, 2017. http://www.electricianschooledu .org/state-by-state-licensing-guide.

Electrician Training Hub. "Electrician Types." Retrieved August 30, 2017. http://electriciantraininghub.com /how-to-become-an-electrician/electrician-types.

Frierson, William. "Interview with an Electrician." College Recruiter, March 13, 2012. https://www.collegerecruiter .com/blog/2012/03/13/interview-with-an-electrician.

Harmon, Daniel E. *A Career as an Electrician*. New York, NY: Rosen Publishing, 2011.

Heibutzki, Ralph. "How to Find Electrical Work." *Career Trend*, July 5, 2017. https://careertrend.com/how-5872385-electrical-work.html.

HomePrep. "Texas Electrical License (Master, Journeyman)." Retrieved September 20, 2017. https://www.contractor-licensing.com/texas/electrical-license.html.

IEC Chesapeake and WECA. *Electrical Pre-apprenticeship and Workforce Development Manual*. Boston, MA: Delmar Cengage Learning, 2013.

Integra Electrical. "5 Most Common Electrical Problems." Integra Electrical 5 Most Common Electrical Problems Comments. Retrieved August 30, 2017. http://www.integraelectrical.co/electrical-problems/5-common-electrical-problems.

Kiplinger. "10 of the Best Jobs for the Future." Yahoo! Finance. April 5, 2013. https://finance.yahoo.com/news/10-of-the-best-jobs-for-the-future-191256480.html.

Jones, Roger. *Real Life Guide: Electrician*. Richmond, UK: Trotman, 2005.

Lytle, Elizabeth Stewart. *Careers as an Electrician*. New York, NY: Rosen Publishing Group, 1999.

Maxwell, Paul. "US Federal Infrastructure Plans: What the Power Sector Needs to Know." *Utility Dive*, April 20, 2017. http://www.utilitydive.com/news/us-federal-infrastructure-plans-what-the-power-sector-needs-to-know/440924.

Nunez, Christina. "One Electrician's Work Makes a Big Difference at a Hospital for Refugees." *National Geographic*, July 14, 2017. http://news.nationalgeographic.com/2017/07/chasing-genius-jordan-hospital-electrician-msf.

Preston, Benjamin. "America's Infrastructure Still Rates No Better Than D+, Engineering Experts Say." *Guardian*, March 9, 2017. https://www.theguardian.com/us-news/2017/mar/09/america-infrastructure-rating-problems-engineers-report.

Rollins, Monique, and Ankur Datta. "Treasury Notes." U.S. Department of the Treasury, December 30, 2016. https://www.treasury.gov/connect/blog/Pages/Importance-of-Infrastructure-Investment-for-Spurring-Growth-.aspx.

Smith, Donna. "What Is Continuing Education?" Study.com. Retrieved September 19, 2017. http://study.com/academy/popular/what-is-continuing-education.html.

Stanford Bulletin. "Electrical Engineering." Retrieved September 18, 2017. http://exploredegrees.stanford.edu/schoolofengineering/electricalengineering.

U.S. Bureau of Labor Statistics. "Electricians." December 17, 2015. https://www.bls.gov/ooh/construction-and-extraction/electricians.htm.

U.S. Bureau of Labor Statistics. "Line Installers and Repairers." December 17, 2015. https://www.bls.gov/ooh/installation-maintenance-and-repair/line-installers-and-repairers.htm#tab-2.

INDEX

ABOUT THE AUTHOR

Jeff Mapua is the author of several books on careers, including *A Career in Customer Service and Tech Support*, *A Career as a Social Media Manager*, and *Making the Most of Crowdfunding*. Mapua has a degree in mathematics from the University of Texas at Austin. He lives in Dallas, Texas, with his wife, Ruby.

PHOTO CREDITS

Cover, p. 3 Pressmaster/Shutterstock.com; pp. 6–7 Reza Estakhrian /The Image Bank/Getty Images; p. 10 Robin Bartholick/Corbis /Getty Images; p. 11 © iStockphoto.com/rahan1991; p. 13 Noi1990 /Shutterstock.com; p. 15 Andrey_Popov/Shutterstock.com; p. 19 The Washington Post/Getty Images; p. 22 Chutima Chaochaiya /Shutterstock.com; pp. 24, 54 Bloomberg/Getty Images; p. 26 Kijja Pruchyathamkorn/Shutterstock.com; p. 30 Phovoir /Shutterstock.com; p. 31 Andrew Aitchison/In Pictures /Getty Images; p. 34 Akimov Igor/Shutterstock.com; p. 36 nd3000/Shutterstock.com; p. 39 ©iStockphoto.com /Daisy-Daisy; p. 41 NetPhotos/Alamy Stock Photo; p. 46 Kent Weakley /Shutterstock.com; p. 48 ah_fotobox/Shutterstock.com; p. 50 Marcel Derweduwen/Shutterstock.com; p. 56 michaeljung/ Shutterstock.com; p. 59 Vladislav Kireychev/Shutterstock.com; p. 60 U.S. Navy/Getty Images; p. 62 miker/Shutterstock.com; interior pages background (electric wires) ndquang/Shutterstock.com.

Design: Nelson Sá; Layout: Nicole Russo-Duca; Editor: Phil Wolny; Photo Researcher: Sherri Jackson